Understanding Economics

Monika Davies

Consultants

Crystal Hahm, M.A.Ed., Ed.M.
Tustin Unified School District

Bijan Kazerooni, M.A.
Chapman University

Publishing Credits

Rachelle Cracchiolo, M.S.Ed., *Publisher*
Conni Medina, M.A.Ed., *Managing Editor*
Emily R. Smith, M.A.Ed., *Series Developer*
June Kikuchi, *Content Director*
Susan Daddis, M.A.Ed., *Editor*
Courtney Roberson, *Senior Graphic Designer*

Image Credits: p.8 Maryland State Archives, Huntingfield Collection, MSA SC 1399-1-101; p.9 Chronicle/Alamy; p.10 North Wind Picture Archives/Alamy; p.11, 32 North Wind Picture Archives; p.23 Rena Schild/Shutterstock; p.24 MaximImages archive/Alamy; p.26 Glasshouse Images/Alamy; p.27 (center) Taina Sohlman/Shutterstock; all other images from iStock and/or Shutterstock.

Library of Congress Cataloging-in-Publication Data

Names: Davies, Monika, author.
Title: Understanding economics / Monika Davies.
Description: Huntington Beach, CA : Teacher Created Materials, [2019] | Includes index.
Identifiers: LCCN 2017053308 (print) | LCCN 2017056800 (ebook) | ISBN 9781425825638 | ISBN 9781425825218 (pbk.)
Subjects: LCSH: Economics. | United States--Economic conditions.
Classification: LCC HB71 (ebook) | LCC HB71 .D295 2019 (print) | DDC 330--dc23
LC record available at https://lccn.loc.gov/2017053308

Teacher Created Materials

5301 Oceanus Drive
Huntington Beach, CA 92649-1030
www.tcmpub.com

ISBN 978-1-4258-2521-8

© 2018 Teacher Created Materials, Inc.
Printed in China
Nordica.012019.CA21801586

Table of Contents

What Is Economics?

When you think of economics, what comes to mind? If you said "money" you are on the right track. Economics is a big word. It has a complex meaning. It is the study of two important points. First, it looks at the process of making and selling goods and services. Then, it studies how people spend the money they make.

Every day, people make choices. Should we have apple juice or orange juice? Should we buy a book or movie tickets? These decisions are economic choices. And these choices affect more than just us. They also affect how our community grows and changes.

The History of Economics

The study of economics goes back to ancient times. Aristotle, a Greek thinker and writer, was born in 384 BC. He wrote that people had simple needs and endless wants. He believed that people should trade to meet their needs.

Statue of Aristotle

Each community has its own economy. This is the system in which goods and services are bought and sold. Goods are items you can see and touch. They can be things such as food, clothes, or phones. Services are actions that someone does for others. A service can be a plumber fixing pipes. Or it might be a bus driver taking people around town.

Every day, people buy and sell goods and services. These actions **fuel** local economies. But what is bought and sold has changed over time. Some goods and services are the same. Others are new. These changes direct the economy.

Hello, Technology

Technology has completely changed our lives. We once went to stores to shop. Now, we shop online. Technology has influenced what we buy and sell while also changing how we buy and sell goods and services.

America's First Economies

In 1607, the first English colony was established in America. It was in Jamestown, Virginia. Settlers arrived from England. They started to build their lives in the new colony. There was **fertile** land. And there was plenty of food for all. Yet, less than half of the settlers survived.

More settlers were sent over. And again, few survived. People were starving. British leaders were confused. How could the settlers be hungry with so much food available? They sent Sir Thomas Dale to find out. Dale was a navy commander. He would be the leader of the new colony.

Jamestown

This map of Virginia was drawn in the early 1600s.

Dale arrived in 1611. When he came, Jamestown needed help. People were hungry but not everyone was working hard. He soon learned one reason why. All the food was shared. Everyone received the same amount, no matter how much their farm grew. There was no **incentive** to grow more.

These are the ruins from the original church tower at Jamestown.

Economics at Work

The colonists were very poor. Then, they found a way to make money selling tobacco. They sold a lot of it to England. The colonists also traded. American Indians gave them corn and furs. In return, the American Indians got tobacco. The economy of the colony improved.

The settlers needed to work toward a future. Dale had a solution. Each man was given three acres of land. The land was now his private property. Any food farmed or found on the land was his to keep. Settlers could also trade or sell anything they grew or hunted.

People knew if they worked hard, they would **prosper**. In a short time, they had more crops. Trade was encouraged.

Jamestown settlers

Soon, the settlers looked for other items to trade. They learned new skills. Some men became blacksmiths. Others became carpenters. **Innovation** was encouraged. This led to new goods and services. The market grew.

The settlers established the first economies. Private property is still a vital part of the United States. That is also true for innovation. These two principles help grow strong economies.

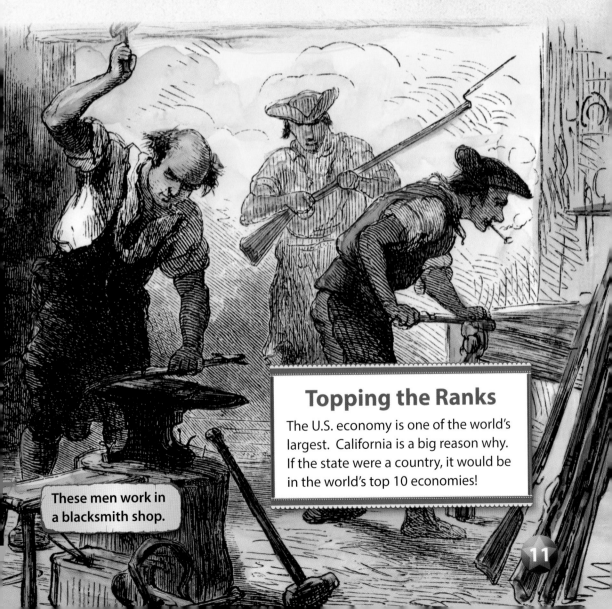

These men work in a blacksmith shop.

Topping the Ranks

The U.S. economy is one of the world's largest. California is a big reason why. If the state were a country, it would be in the world's top 10 economies!

Your Role in the Economy

We all play a part in our local economy. We buy goods and services. And we choose the goods and services to invest in.

Everything bought and sold comes with a benefit and a cost. A benefit is something gained. A cost is something lost. We weigh both when making choices.

What Is a Trade-off?

A trade-off is when we take less of one thing to gain more of something else. Every choice we make is a trade-off. For example, you might earn an allowance. You have a choice to save your money for a while to buy a video game or buy snacks now. You really want the video game. But the snacks in the store look good.

One example is when we pick food to eat. Every day, there are people who decide to buy a slice of pizza. This is a choice. They think about the benefits and cost. The benefit of buying a slice is that it will fill an empty stomach. But pizzas come with a price tag. The cost is the money paid for the pizza. If someone buys a pizza slice, they see the benefits outweighing the cost.

Human Capital

Your role in the economy is more than your buying choices. You have skills and knowledge. These are called human capital. They can change over time. Going to school is one way to build your human capital.

The human mind is an important tool. It solves problems. And it makes decisions. This is needed in every line of work.

Population Riches

Many people call California home. Over 39 million people live there. More people live in the Golden State than in all of Canada! And they all help drive the state's economy.

In school, you learn many subjects. You read and write. You practice adding and subtracting. You learn how to solve problems. It helps grow your skill set. Your hard work as a student develops your abilities. This enhances your human capital.

Your work in school helps build your future. Maybe you will be an **entrepreneur** (ahn-truh-pruh-NUHR). Or you might be a skilled worker in an industry you love. Either way, your skills help your community. When you succeed, so does your community. Your success helps grow the economy.

Factors of Production

Goods and services are a big part of economies. But they do not pop out of thin air! They must be produced. Production of goods and services relies on four "building blocks." These are the factors of production.

land   labor

capital   entrepreneurship

Land: Natural Resources

The first factor of production is land. But land is more than the soil under our feet. It includes any natural resource. A natural resource is something found in nature. And it is something people can use to create goods and services.

The list of natural resources is long. Water is one. Fruit plucked from a tree also counts. Even wind is a natural resource!

A "Fruitful" Exchange

Many states have local farmers' markets. Farmers set up booths or stands. They sell directly to people, not to a store. And these markets aren't just limited to fruits and vegetables. Other farmers will sell fresh meats, honey, cheeses, and eggs.

Labor: Human Resources

The second factor of production is labor. This is the work that people do to help produce goods and services. It is also known as *human resources*.

Think of where you live. Examples of labor are everywhere. Who cuts your hair? A barber or hairdresser cuts and styles hair. How does a garden come to life? A gardener takes care of plants and lawns. How are purchases processed? A cashier rings it up. How is a painting made? A painter uses a brush to color the art. These all show labor in action!

Here, There, Everywhere!

Have you ever looked at the tag on your shirt? You may have seen a label that says, "Made in China." Some of the goods you buy are made in your local community. Others are crafted in another part of the country. And, some goods are created **abroad**. The goods we buy come from all around the world.

MADE IN CHINA
HECHO EN CHINA

Capital Resources

The third factor of production is capital. Capital comes in many shapes and sizes. It could be tools. Or, it might be machinery. Buildings also count. Capital is different for every worker. A tool for a builder is a hammer. But a tool for an artist is a pencil.

Consider a barbershop. A barber's tool is a pair of scissors. That tool is capital. The barbershop is located in a building. The building is also capital. All this is needed for the barber shop to run. The scissors and the building did not come from nature. They were made to make other goods or provide services. That is why they are known as capital resources.

Changing Economy

In the twenty-first century, some companies are spending less on capital. They are spending more on things that can't be seen or touched. For example, there are now people selling goods on the Internet. People don't have to go to a store. They can order online.

Entrepreneurship

The fourth factor of production is the most important. It is entrepreneurship. This is when people innovate.

Innovation takes place in all lines of work. First, a person or team starts with an idea. Then, they **pool** their resources. These include land, labor, and capital. Their goals are to make goods or services that help people or make lives easier. Their ideas might also make a **profit**.

All entrepreneurs have a story. They might be a group of bakers selling cupcakes. Or they can be a team running an online store. They can even be different companies working on the same products. For example, many companies have changed how mobile phones are made.

Entrepreneurs go after their goals. They find the resources they need. This helps them to succeed. When their business grows, it helps the economy grow, too.

Changes have made mobile phones faster.

Oprah Winfrey is a famous entrepreneur in television, film, and magazines.

The Risk Takers

Entrepreneurs are known for their risk-taking spirits! Many start with very little. Yet, they have big dreams. Most start their own business. They take big financial risks to follow their dreams. Famous entrepreneurs include Oprah Winfrey, Steve Jobs, and Walt Disney. Can you think of others?

Jake the Baker

The factors of production work together to produce goods and services. Let's look at an example to see how production comes together.

Jake has perfected the art of making pecan pies. This year, he has decided to open his own shop. First, he needs resources. His recipe calls for certain ingredients. These include pecans and eggs. Both are natural resources. Next, he buys a new mixer. He also chooses a shop where he can sell his pies. These are capital resources. Finally, he hires someone to ring up purchases. Jake will bake. His new hire will serve. They all provide labor, which is human resources.

On their own, these resources would not produce a good or a service. But Jake the entrepreneur has mixed these resources together. Now, he has a business that sells goods: pecan pies! This is one way the factors of production create a recipe for success.

Jake rolls and shapes pie crust.

A Key Ingredient

Jake's recipe for success has another key ingredient: **private property rights**. The first English settlers had the right to own, buy, and sell land. That is still true. Now you are free to do what you want with your property. This allows Jake to buy a shop to sell his pecan pies. His rights give him the freedom to pursue his dream.

What the Future Holds

America is still growing. Much has changed since the first settlers arrived. We now live in a modern era. We travel by car, not horseback. Skyscrapers reach for the sun. The Internet sits at our fingertips.

The world is always changing. And that is true for our economies, too. But some things remain the same. We make choices about what we buy and sell. These choices drive our economies. Looking at what guides our choices is crucial. Our decisions help shape our community's future. Understanding our role in the economy is one way to keep the future looking bright.

The horse and buggy was a popular way to travel in the late 1800s to early 1900s.

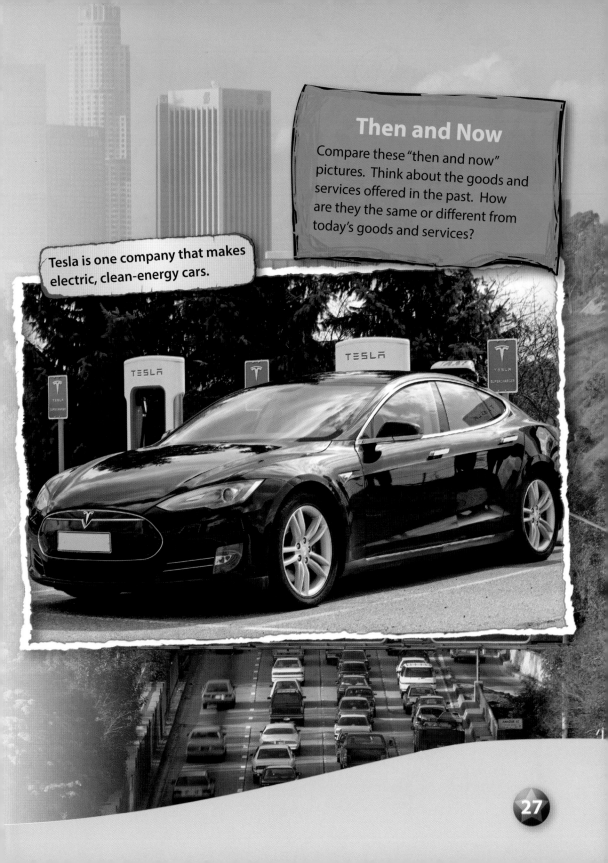

Then and Now

Compare these "then and now" pictures. Think about the goods and services offered in the past. How are they the same or different from today's goods and services?

Tesla is one company that makes electric, clean-energy cars.

Write It!

Many entrepreneurs start with dreams. They have ideas that put their resources to new uses.

Imagine you work for the school newspaper. You are asked to write an article about a local entrepreneur or business owner.

Set up a time for the interview. Have a list of questions prepared. Here are two examples to get you started. How did you come up with your ideas? What was the hardest part of getting started? Think of two more questions you would like to ask.

Conduct the interview and write the article. Include a headline and date. Share with your friends or family.

STREET FOOD

GLUTEN FREE

LA AUTÉNTICA
COMIDA
DE LOS

WE
LOVE

PRUEBA NUESTROS

→PAN DE QUESO ·3,5€

Bon

Profit!!

Glossary

abroad—in a foreign country

entrepreneur—a person who starts a business to help people or make life easier in some way

fertile—capable of supporting the growth of many plants

fuel—to give strength to something

incentive—something that gives a person a purpose to work harder

innovation—a new idea or way to do something

pool—to put people, supplies, and money together to make a product

private property rights—a person's right to own property and decide how the property is used

profit—money a business makes after all the costs and workers are paid

prosper—become healthy and strong

Index

Your Turn!

Business Know-How

Early settlers started businesses based on needs in their communities. Think of needs in your neighborhood. For example, someone might need a pet sitter. Make a flyer advertising a good or service you can provide. Include the name of your business and details your neighbors will need about it.